CRIME AND DETECTION

FAMOUS TRIALS

Crime and Detection series

- Criminal Terminology
- Cyber Crime
- Daily Prison Life
- Death Row and Capital Punishment
- Domestic Crime
- Famous Prisons
- Famous Trials
- Forensic Science
- Government Intelligence Agencies
- Hate Crimes
- The History and Methods of Torture
- The History of Punishment
- International Terrorism
- Major Unsolved Crimes
- Organized Crime
- Protecting Yourself Against Criminals
- Race and Crime
- Serial Murders
- The United States Justice System
- The War Against Drugs

CRIME AND DETECTION

FAMOUS TRIALS

JOAN LOCK

MASON CREST PUBLISHERS
www.masoncrest.com

Mason Crest Publishers Inc.
370 Reed Road
Broomall, PA 19008
(866) MCP-BOOK (toll free)
www.masoncrest.com

13 12 11 10 09 08 07 06   10 9 8 7 6 5 4 3 2

Library of Congress Cataloging-in-Publication Data

Lock, Joan.
  Famous trials / Joan Lock.
    v. cm. — (Crime and detection)
  Includes bibliographical references and index.
  Contents: How trials become famous — Leopold and Loeb: the playboy killers — The German
carpenter — Sacco and Vanzetti: a case that rocked the world — John George Haigh: the acid-
bath murderer — The trials of Dr. Sheppard.
  ISBN 1-59084-381-9 (hardcover)
  1. Trials—Juvenile literature. 2. Trials—United States—Juvenile literature. [1. Trials.] I. Title.
II. Series.

K542.L63 2003
347.73'7—dc21
                                        2003000478

Editorial and design by
Amber Books Ltd.
Bradley's Close
74–77 White Lion Street
London N1 9PF
www.amberbooks.co.uk

Project Editor: Michael Spilling
Design: Floyd Sayers
Picture Research: Natasha Jones

Printed and bound in Malaysia

Picture credits
Amber Books: 25, 72, 73; Corbis: 50, 55, 56; The Picture Desk, Kobal
Collection: 85; Mary Evans Picture Library: 17, 18, 61; PA Photos: 6,
59; Popperfoto: 36(b), 39, 49; Topham Picturepoint: 8, 10, 11, 13, 14,
15, 22, 26, 27, 28, 31, 33, 34, 36(c), 41, 42, 44, 45, 46, 47, 52, 54,
58, 62–63, 64, 66, 67, 69, 74, 77, 78, 81, 82, 84, 87, 88, 89.
Front cover: (Clockwise from top) Topham Picturepoint, Corbis,
Topham Picturepoint, Corbis, Topham Picturepoint.

CONTENTS

Introduction 7

How Trials Become Famous 9

Leopold and Loeb: The Playboy Killers 23

The German Carpenter 35

Sacco and Vanzetti: A Case That 51
Rocked the World

John George Haigh: The Acid-Bath Murderer 63

The Trials of Dr. Sheppard 75

Glossary 90

Chronology 92

Further Information 94

Index 96

Introduction

From the moment in the Book of Genesis when Cain's envy of his brother Abel erupted into violence, crime has been an inescapable feature of human life. Every society ever known has had its own sense of how things ought to be, its deeply held views on how men and women should behave. Yet in every age there have been individuals ready to break these rules for their own advantage: they must be resisted if the community is to thrive.

This exciting and vividly illustrated new series sets out the history of crime and detection from the earliest times to the present day, from the empires of the ancient world to the towns and cities of the 21st century. From the commandments of the great religions to the theories of modern psychologists, it considers changing attitudes toward offenders and their actions. Contemporary crime is examined in its many different forms: everything from racial hatred to industrial espionage, from serial murder to drug trafficking, from international terrorism to domestic violence.

The series looks, too, at the work of those men and women entrusted with the task of overseeing and maintaining the law, from judges and court officials to police officers and other law enforcement agents. The tools and techniques at their disposal are described and vividly illustrated, and the ethical issues they face concisely and clearly explained.

All in all, the *Crime and Detection* series provides a comprehensive and accessible account of crime and detection, in theory and in practice, past and present.

CHARLIE FULLER
Executive Director, International Association of Undercover Officers

Left: On November 10, 1997, British au pair Louise Woodward, 19, listens as a judge reduces her conviction for the murder of a child within her care to one of manslaughter. The Woodward case received enormous publicity throughout the United States and the world.

How Trials Become Famous

There are several reasons why certain trials become famous. Those involved may already be well known, as in the Lindbergh kidnapping. The crime itself might be unusual, as with that of John George Haigh, who dissolved his victims in acid, or Dr. Sheppard, whose story seemed so unlikely. In the case of the playboy killers, Leopold and Loeb, it was most certainly their repulsive motive that drew so much attention.

Lingering doubt about the guilt of the accused features strongly in three of these famous trials—those of Dr. Sheppard, Bruno Hauptmann, and Sacco and Vanzetti. In fact, feelings about the treatment of Sacco and Vanzetti, and the politics this involved, led to rioting all around the world.

News of the latest scientific methods also helps draw attention. The science of **ballistics** played a part in the case of Sacco and Vanzetti, and typewriter **forensics** was used with Leopold and Loeb.

New technology, combined with an exciting transatlantic chase, ensured that the trial of Dr. Crippen, known as the "cellar murderer," would become one of the most famous ever.

DR. CRIPPEN: THE CELLAR MURDERER

Early in 1910, the British Music Hall Guild was surprised to receive a letter from Cora Crippen. In this letter, Mrs. Crippen resigned from her

Left: Former American football player O.J. Simpson, here with British public relations executive Max Clifford, appears at the Oxford University Union on May 14, 1996, after he had been acquitted on the charge of murdering his wife and her friend.

This illustration depicts the arrest of Dr. Crippen by Canadian police on his arrival at Quebec, Canada, as he attempts to alight undetected from the SS *Montrose*. The "boy" on the left in the sailor cap is his mistress, Ethel le Neve.

Chief Inspector Walter Dew of Scotland Yard (in the dark bowler hat) escorts Dr. Crippen down the gangway following his arrest. Huge crowds greeted their arrival back in England.

membership and stated that she was leaving for the United States to take care of a sick relative. Shortly afterward, her husband, Dr. Hawley Harvey Crippen, told her friends that his wife was seriously ill with pneumonia.

Dr. Crippen and Cora were American citizens who lived in England at 39 Hilldrop Crescent in North London. He worked as a patent medicine salesman, while she was trying to make her way as a music hall singer under the name of Belle Elmore. Their marriage was not a happy one. The flamboyant Cora took lovers, and Dr. Crippen began an affair with his assistant, Ethel le Neve.

Soon, Dr. Crippen had more bad news for Cora's friends. He said that she had died while still in the United States. Cora's friends noticed, however, that his period of mourning was short; it had not taken long for Ethel to move in with him. And soon after that she was even seen wearing some of Cora's jewelry and furs.

Most of Cora's friends had never liked the doctor, and they now became suspicious. They made inquiries with shipping lines, but no record could be found of Cora ever having made the trip to the United States. So they went to the police.

Chief Inspector Walter Dew of Scotland Yard was sent to see Dr. Crippen, who soon confessed that he had not been telling the truth. Cora was not dead; she had just left him. He had told the stories about her being ill and dying so as to avoid embarrassment and scandal. A search of the house in Hilldrop Crescent revealed nothing suspicious.

Two days later, the Chief Inspector went back to ask a few more questions, only to discover that the doctor had chosen to take a leave of absence from his firm. His house was now deserted. This time, police made a more thorough search of the premises and, after digging in the coal cellar, they found human remains.

A CAPTAIN'S CURIOSITY PAYS OFF

A warrant was immediately taken out for the arrest of the "the cellar murderer and his accomplice." Photographs and descriptions of the fugitive pair, Crippen and Ethel, were sent to police forces throughout Europe and North America and also published in newspapers. Ethel was reported to be nice-looking, quiet, and ladylike, and to have light brown hair and large, gray-blue eyes.

Four days after the warrant was issued, Captain Henry Kendall of the SS *Montrose*, which had just left Antwerp for Quebec, became curious about two of his passengers. Mr. John Robinson resembled the newspaper photograph of Dr. Crippen, despite having shaved off his moustache and starting to grow a beard. He was also short—only five feet, three inches in height—just like Dr. Crippen. Mr. Robinson's sixteen-year-old "son" had a

This photograph shows Ethel le Neve, dressed in boy's clothes. After her acquittal, she emigrated to Canada, but she returned to England in 1916 and later married an accountant who was said to resemble Dr. Crippen.

The SS *Montrose,* on which Dr. Crippen and Ethel le Neve fled to Quebec. The inset shows Captain Henry Kendall, who became suspicious of the affectionate pair.

rather odd appearance. He wore an ill-fitting suit, was described as being "very tight about the hips," and seemed somewhat feminine in his manners.

The SS *Montrose* had been fitted with the latest wireless telegraphy equipment. Captain Kendall sent a long message back to his shipping company in Liverpool describing his passengers and his suspicions. Scotland Yard was informed, and, as a result, Chief Inspector Dew boarded a faster boat, the SS *Laurentic.* He reached Canada ahead of the fugitives and was there to meet them on their arrival. Ethel is reported to have screamed and fainted at the sight of the policeman. The case caused a sensation, and back in England, huge crowds stood at the dock to greet the arrival of the ship that carried Crippen and Ethel le Neve.

At the trial, Dr. Crippen still insisted that Cora had left him and that the remains found in his coal cellar must be that of someone else. Obviously,

Dr. Crippen was the first murderer to be captured with the aid of the wireless telegraph invented by Marconi in 1896. "Handcuffs London" was Scotland Yard's telegraphic address.

he said, they had been put there either before he came to the house or without his knowledge while he was there.

The question of whether the body was that of Cora hinged on a scar on a portion of the skin found. If it was from the leg, as the forensic experts for the defense claimed, the remains were not Cora's. If it was from the stomach, as the prosecution insisted, it was Cora.

INCRIMINATING FORENSIC EVIDENCE

Dr. Bernard Spilsbury, the prosecution's authority on scars, insisted the scar was from the stomach. He proved such a convincing witness that he caused one of the defense experts during Crippen's trial to change his mind. In fact, Spilsbury was to become Britain's most famous forensic witness. Indeed, some complained that his confident manner convinced juries he was incapable of making a mistake.

The case against Dr. Crippen was strengthened by more forensic evidence. A drug, known as hyoscine, had been found in the organs of the body. In fact, there was enough there to prove fatal. It was also shown that two weeks before Cora was last seen alive, Dr. Crippen had bought a quantity of the drug—supposedly to treat his patients.

Then there was the fact that Crippen was short of money and Cora had been threatening to leave, taking hers with her. Shortly after her disappearance, he had pawned some of his wife's jewelry.

But the evidence that finally sank Dr. Crippen was the label on a scrap of pajama jacket in which the remains had been wrapped. A jacket was missing from one of Crippen's pairs of pajamas. He claimed they had been bought as far back as 1905 and that the jacket had gone missing a long time ago. Inquiries with the store who supplied them showed that the label had come into use only in 1909.

It took the jury just 27 minutes to find Dr. Crippen guilty of murder, and he was sentenced to death. Shortly after he was hanged, his attorney, Arthur Newton, sold Crippen's "confession" to a newspaper. This was

THE MURDERER TAWELL (1845)

John Tawell was a crook, who, at the early age of 20, was transported to Sydney, in Australia, as a common criminal. After his release, he grew rich dealing in medicines and whalebone. On his return to England, he adopted the dress of a Quaker and also became known for his charitable works.

He installed his young mistress, Sarah Hart, in a house in Slough. But when he married for the second time, he was afraid that his new wife would learn about his other woman.

Following one of his visits to Slough, Sarah was found writhing on the ground. She died soon afterward. Her screams had attracted the attention of neighbors, who saw a man dressed as a Quaker leaving the house. He was later spotted boarding a train for Paddington. A telegram sent ahead of him ensured that he was arrested upon arrival.

Sarah, it was subsequently found, had been poisoned with prussic acid. A pharmacist came forward to say he had sold the poison to Tawell on the morning of the murder. This evidence proved damning, and Tawell was found guilty and executed.

found to be a forgery, however, and Newton himself ended up in prison.

Ethel le Neve was tried separately and **acquitted**. Early accounts of the case tended to portray Dr. Crippen, "the mild murderer," as an amiable and kindly man, and Ethel le Neve as sweetly innocent. Cora, who was the victim after all, was portrayed as a screaming, slovenly, malicious woman. Some even claimed that the hyoscine was given to her accidentally in an overdose and that Crippen had simply wanted to send his wife to sleep while he entertained Ethel.

This illustration shows a French railway telegraph office. The electric telegraph was invented in 1837. The murderer John Tawell was caught via the first public link, between Slough and Paddington Station, shortly after it opened in 1843.

The reality is probably that while Cora was admittedly volatile, unfaithful, and domineering—as well as given to bouts of screaming temper tantrums at home—she was also lively, good-natured, and likeable. The fact that she had good friends who cared enough to make sure her disappearance did not go unnoticed certainly seems proof of that.

ANOTHER TRANSATLANTIC DASH

Dr. Crippen was not the first murderer to be captured after a transatlantic dash by the British police. In Victorian times, many British criminals thought their best way to escape justice was to flee to the United States, as did Franz Muller in 1864.

Muller became the first person to murder someone on a railroad when he killed Thomas Briggs on a London train. He stole £5 and the man's gold watch, then picked up his victim's top hat in mistake for his own.

He sold the watch chain to a jeweler named De'Ath, who later told police that the seller seemed foreign, probably German. A cab driver came forward to say that the stubby hat that the murderer had left behind was similar to two that he himself had bought. He had kept one and given the other to a tailor named Franz Muller. The cab driver not only knew where Muller lived, but he also had a photograph of him. By the time police reached Muller's lodgings, however, he had gone.

His landlady said that her kind, mild-mannered lodger had often told her of his wish to move to the United States and that suddenly he had found enough money to go. She showed police a postcard he had sent just before he left for New York on a sailing ship, the *Victoria*.

A transatlantic telegraph cable now linked the two countries, but it was not possible to send messages to ships at sea at this time. However, the new steamships were much quicker than sailing ships. Scotland Yard Detective Inspector Richard Tanner, his Detective Sergeant, the jeweler De'Ath, and the cab driver boarded the fast SS *City of Manchester*, which got them to New York three weeks ahead of Muller.

MARIA MANNING: THE WOMAN WHO KILLED BLACK SATIN (1849)

Friends raised the alarm in 1849 for another victim, as alert friends of Cora Crippen were to do some 60 years later. A wealthy customs man by the name of Patrick O'Connor was missing, and his friends insisted that the police investigate. They knew that Patrick was in the habit of visiting a former girlfriend, Mrs. Maria Manning, and her husband Frederick, who lived in Bermondsey in South London. In fact, he had last been seen while on his way to have supper with them.

Police were slow to act, but eventually made several visits. The charming, Swiss-born Maria swore that O'Connor had never arrived on the appointed evening. Similarly to the Crippen case, when police visited again, they found the house empty. One of the policemen noticed that the mortar around the kitchen flagstones was damp. He later declared, "This arrested my attention." Under the flagstones, they found the body of Patrick O'Connor. There was a bullet in his brain and extensive fractures to the back of his skull.

Inquiries revealed that two passengers by the name of Manning had boarded the American passenger and cargo boat SS *Victoria* at London docks on the very day that the body was discovered. A telegram was sent to two detectives who were at Portsmouth docks searching ships bound for the United States.

They were instructed to stop the SS *Victoria* as it passed along the English Channel heading for the Atlantic. However, this was easier said than done: the ship refused to respond to signals telling it to heave to. The Royal Navy came to the rescue by lending the detectives a high-speed steam yacht in which they were able to give chase.

It took four and a half hours for them to catch up, but when they boarded the ship, they found the two Mannings were not Maria and Frederick after all. They were an innocent mother and daughter lying seasick on their bunks.

Later, when Edinburgh Police detained a foreign woman who had been selling suspect railroad shares, the now-extended telegraph network was used to flash Maria's description to the Scottish force. A distinctive scar on her face gave away her identity, and an arrest was made. Frederick Manning was tracked down to Jersey in the Channel Islands.

Other available evidence against the pair was overwhelming. Both were found guilty and sentenced to death. Maria, who was thought to be the mastermind behind the crime, wore a black satin dress for her public execution. The material instantly went out of fashion.

THE EVIDENCE AGAINST MULLER

The stolen gold watch was found on Muller's person. Along with this, he had in his possession a silk top hat, which Muller had shortened to resemble his own. **Extradition** proved slow and difficult. The American authorities were angry with Britain at that time because they were helping the rebellious South run the blockade in the Civil War. Eventually, however, the police returned to London with their prisoner.

Franz Muller swore his innocence, but inexplicably confessed just before he was hanged. For a time, "Muller cut-down" hats became highly fashionable—quite the opposite of what occurred in the case of Maria Manning (see box, left).

Leopold and Loeb: The Playboy Killers

It was the motive as much as the crime itself that horrified the world when 19-year-old Nathan Leopold and 18-year-old Richard Loeb stood trial for murder in Chicago in 1924. These two brilliant and wealthy young men had killed 14-year-old Bobby Franks just for fun and to prove how superior they were.

Both of them were sons of prominent Chicago families. The pair had met when Leopold was 14, and they soon became inseparable. Indulged with every luxury, they grew bored and began to commit acts of vandalism and petty theft. Eventually, they set about planning the ultimate crime—the perfect murder.

Realizing that their own cars would be identified, they decided to rent one. Leopold checked into Chicago's Morrison Hotel as Morton D. Ballard, a salesman from Peoria, then went to a car rental agency, gave the same name, and picked out a sedan for later use.

Leopold had a typewriter that Loeb had stolen from the University of Michigan. They decided to use this for the ransom note they intended to send after they had kidnapped and killed their victim. The typewriter would not be traceable to them, and a ransom note would divert suspicion from them because they clearly had all the money they needed.

Then they assembled their murder pack: rope, a heavy chisel to use as a

Left: This photograph shows Nathan Leopold on his release from Stateville Penitentiary, Illinois, after he had served 33 years for the slaying of Bobby Franks. He subsequently wrote a book, *Life Plus 99 Years*, about his experiences.

weapon, strips of cloth to use as a gag, a car blanket to cover the body, and hydrochloric acid to destroy the victim's identity. They bound the handle of the chisel with string to give a better grip, picked up the rental car, and went out looking for a victim. It had to be someone small, they had decided, because neither of them was particularly strong.

A VICTIM IS SELECTED

They found young Bobby Franks, a friend of Loeb's younger brother, and invited him for a ride. He was soon overpowered and gagged. His skull was fractured with four blows from the chisel, and his body was stuffed in a pipe near a culvert in a drained swamp.

A call was made to Bobby Franks' parents telling them that their son had been kidnapped. They were told to expect ransom notes and warned that if the police were brought in, Bobby would be killed.

A ransom note signed by "George Johnson" and demanding $10,000 was delivered to the parents the next day. It assured them the boy was alive and well. Soon afterward, however, his body was discovered.

Loeb and Leopold had second thoughts about the typewriter. They broke it up and threw the pieces into a lagoon. Then Nathan Leopold went into hiding, staying in his room at home. Richard Loeb, the dominant, sociable one of the two, joined the hunt for the killers. He could not resist offering assistance and advice to the police—a not uncommon reaction of murderers eager to thumb their noses at "dumb cops."

Objects connected with the crime began turning up. Pieces of the typewriter were recovered along with the bloodstained chisel, as well as a pair of glasses. The spectacles were found near the body and proved to have unusual features. The manufacturers told police that they had made only three pairs: one for a lawyer who had gone to Europe, a second for a lady who was wearing them when police arrived to interview her, and a third for Nathan Leopold.

When police questioned him, Leopold claimed that he must have dropped them while he was watching birds near the culvert some time before and that he often went there. When the boys were asked what they had been doing on the night in question, they claimed they had been out in Leopold's car looking for girls (in fact, both were homosexual).

BUT WHERE IS THE MOTIVE?

There was initial disbelief that wealthy and talented young men with their eminent social position would need to kidnap a young boy. However, police soon realized that Leopold and Loeb were among their prime suspects.

Meanwhile, two reporters from the *Chicago Daily News* began talking to friends of Leopold and Loeb. One of them said he was part of a law study

Police search for and discover the body of Bobby Franks on the outskirts of Chicago. Leopold's spectacles were also found there. He claimed to have lost them while birdwatching.

Here, police officers arrest Nathan Leopold and Richard Loeb for the murder of 14-year-old Bobby Franks. Because they were too wealthy to need the ransom money, the two teenagers imagined that no one would suspect them.

group that met at the Leopold mansion. To copy out study notes, Leopold normally used a large Hammond typewriter, but on one occasion had produced a small, portable typewriter.

The student still had some of these notes. A typewriter expert examined them and declared that they had been typed on the same machine as that used for the ransom note. Leopold claimed it belonged to first one, and

TELLTALE TYPEWRITERS

During the early days of typewriting, it was thought that since typewriting was a mechanical process, no one would be able to tell who had sent a typewritten threat or ransom note.

However, investigators soon realized that different makes had different styles of type and spacing, and that wear and tear caused each machine to develop its own characteristics.

Certain letters became less distinct because of wear or damage, and there could be a variation in blackness as the result of a patchy carbon ribbon or a worn or dirty roller. Each typewriter had its own distinct fingerprint, which could help bring a criminal to justice—as in the case of Leopold and Loeb.

then another of the other students, who was in Europe. Then he claimed it was still in his house somewhere, but a search failed to uncover the portable typewriter.

The final piece of the puzzle fell into place when Sven Englund, the Leopold chauffeur, was brought in for questioning. He told police that Leopold and Loeb had definitely not been driving around in Leopold's flashy, red Willys-Knight car on the evening of the murder, as they had claimed. He had been working on it in the garage trying to fix its noisy brakes. Police tracked down the car used for the kidnapping, and Leopold was identified as the Morton D. Ballard who had rented the vehicle.

TRICKED INTO CONFESSING

The killers were deceived into confessing. Police used the old trick of telling each of them that the other had confessed and put all the blame on him. Each then claimed that it was the other one who had actually committed the murder. From their statements, it seemed most likely that Loeb struck the fatal blows, but they were both charged with the murder.

The famous criminal lawyer Clarence Darrow saved them from the electric chair by emphasizing their youth, describing them as mentally abnormal, and making a prolonged attack on **capital punishment**.

Mrs. Mabel Tattershaw, a mother of two with a husband in prison, became the victim of the desire of Herbert Mills to commit the perfect, undiscovered murder.

FORENSIC EVIDENCE

Hairs found at the scene of a crime can reveal:

• Whether they came from a human or animal.

• If animal, which species.

• If human, which race.

• The part of the body they came from.

• The DNA of the person from which they came.

• Whether they had been pulled out or fell out naturally.

• If they had been bleached, dyed, permed, straightened, lacquered, or gelled.

• Whether the victim has been poisoned with arsenic and, if so, how much.

• Whether the hair is the same as that of a suspect.

• Even if the root is not attached, mitochondrial DNA (which we receive only from our mothers) may be extracted.

They were each sentenced to life imprisonment plus 99 years on the kidnapping charge. In 1936, Richard Loeb was murdered by a fellow prisoner, who claimed to have been resisting his homosexual advances. Nathan Leopold was released on parole in 1958. He married in 1961, and died in 1971.

Another youth who wanted to commit the perfect murder was 19-year-old Herbert Mills of Nottingham in Northern England.

On August 9, 1951, Mills telephoned a tabloid newspaper, the *News of the World*, claiming to have discovered the body of a woman who had been strangled. He asked to be paid £250 for his "scoop." Staff kept him talking and meanwhile contacted the police. The call was traced and the officers who were sent to the scene found him in the telephone booth still in conversation with the newspaper.

CAUGHT BY A THREAD

- Like hairs, textile fibers often transfer from person to person on close contact.
- Textile fibers can be more easily identified than hairs by comparing them against reference sets kept by forensic science laboratories and with information obtained from the manufacturers.
- Textile fibers divide initially into two groups: natural, such as wool, cotton, and silk, and the many varieties of synthetics.
- Synthetic fibers can be easier to compare because they take up dye more evenly than, for example, cotton.

Mills took them to an orchard in Sherwood Vale, where, he said, he often went to read and write poetry. Here they found the body of 48-year-old Mrs. Mabel Tattershaw, who had been missing from her home since August 3. She appeared to have been battered to death with a blunt instrument. It was not until a **postmortem** was carried out, however, that it was discovered that she had actually been strangled.

Herbert Mills' story and photograph were published in the *News of the World*, and Mills continued to show a great interest in the crime.

ANOTHER MURDER WITHOUT A MOTIVE?

As in the Leopold and Loeb case, the murder seemed motiveless. Mrs. Tattershaw had not been sexually assaulted or robbed. When questioned further by the police, Mills' story began to change. He admitted he had found the body earlier than he had previously claimed and that the marks on her neck had been clear. Eventually, Mills confessed to the murder to the crime reporter of the *News of the World*, who had been told what questions to ask by the police.

DAILY EXPRESS FRIDAY NOVEMBER 23 1962

Mills loses gamble for life

JURY FINDS HIM GUILTY OF ORCHARD MURDER

Express Staff Reporter: Nottingham, Thursday

AT 19, Herbert Leonard Mills was sentenced to death today. He said he was a gambler; he said he was a liar. And a jury of 11 men and one woman decided he was a murderer.

He gambled with his life as calmly as—when he was only 15—he gambled hundreds of pounds in cash. He lost as calmly. He stood, arms folded, beneath a cluster of electric lamps at Nottingham Assizes and heard the sentence. When he was asked if he had anything to say, he replied firmly: "No, nothing."

His father, a miner, was sitting in court. Mills ignored him. He jerked his head and looked up to the crowded public gallery; and then he turned away.

Mills's counsel, Mr. Richard Elwes, K.C., had told the jury: "If you are ever going to see a man who has gambled with his life and is composed"—*Mr. Elwes dropped his voice to a whisper*—"whether he wins or loses, you are seeing one now.

"It is a most unusual murder trial. In one way it is almost unique. . . . There is not one shred of sympathy for this man, and I should be the last to expect it."

'No sadist'

Mills was found guilty of strangling Mrs. Mabel Tattershaw, who was 30 years older than him, in a derelict orchard known as "The Jungle."

Mrs. Tattershaw—her husband is in prison—had two daughters. Mills, who was said to have an aversion to women, met her in a Nottingham cinema the day before she was killed.

In his defence, it was argued that this was a sadistic murder, and Mills was no sadist. Love of the limelight, the jury was told, landed him in the dock.

For Mills said he found the body, and decided to make money by phoning a newspaper before he told the police.

He wrote a confession. In court he said this was bogus, invented to get more money. Yes, he would tell anyone a lie if it was to his benefit. Yes, his desire for money was such that he would stop at nothing.

The prosecution analysed the confession. Twelve facts in it were proved true—and counsel claimed that the rest, dealing with the killing, was also true.

'He was bitter'

Hairs similar to Mills's were found on Mrs. Tattershaw. Fibres under her fingernails matched those in Mills's blue suit. And how odd, said counsel, that the confession fixed the time of the bogus murder at the very time and date it actually happened.

Mills's story about his lies was mentioned to the jury by Mr. Justice Byrne, summing up. Was it to the youth's benefit to tell lies now, if they would get him acquitted? he asked.

All through the four-day trial, Mills's 45-year-old father sat in the front row of the public seats in the court.

He said when it was all over: "The boy was born with his feet turned the wrong way. This meant 13 years' painful treatment. He could never play with other children. He was bitter.

"He had a lot of love for two people: My stepson, who is five, and June Brown." [A nurse to whom Mills wrote poetry from jail.]

£1,600 bet

Mr. Mills went on: "Leonard was mad on gambling. When he was just 17 he won £3,800. He lost it all. Once he backed £1,600 on a horse, but it lost."

IN CELL NEXT TO DEAD WOMAN'S HUSBAND . . .

THE face of Herbert Leonard Mills. . . . When he was first arrested he was put in a cell in Lincoln jail. In the next cell was William Tattershaw, husband of the woman Mills has been found guilty of murdering. Trouble threatened. Whispers passed along the prison "grapevine"—and Tattershaw, serving two years for shopbreaking, was moved to Liverpool jail.

The Pope agrees: The world is billions of years old

Express Staff Reporter

THE Pope made theological history yesterday. In an address to scientists in Rome he agreed with scientific estimates that the world is five billion years old.

That figure, said the Pope, "may seem astounding." But it does not conflict, he explained, with the opening words of Genesis: *In the beginning.*

For those three words mean that of *some time,* at the beginning of time, the world was created. And that was what modern scientists were saying. Said the Pope:—

Creation took place in time. Therefore, there is a Creator

estimate of Old Testament history have fixed the Creation at roughly 6,000 years ago. This was refuted by geologists and other scientists.

In his 6,000-word speech, the Pope touched upon astrophysics, the theory of spiral nebulae, nuclear physics and radioactivity. And on research into the splitting of the atom, he said:—

"Insofar as it contributes to the cause of peace, this is certainly to be inscribed among the glories of our century. But even this atomic [text cut off]

Slimming judge tells man: Lose weight

JUDGE DALE, who has been having trouble with his waist-line, gave some advice yesterday to a man faced with a similar problem. The advice? Take a slimming course.

The man, a 16-stoner, was sued in Westminster County Court by a firm of Dover-street tailors for £44 0s. 6d., the balance of the price of three suits.

He counter-claimed for £66 5s. he had paid to the tailors. He said the suits did not fit, and never had fitted.

Two inches bigger

But the man was measured in court, and his chest, waist and hip measurements were at least two inches bigger than when he ordered the suits.

The man said he had been on the Continent. Then Judge Dale said:—

"I had a month in France a short while ago and, unfortunately, put on nearly six inches round the waist. I am getting it off now."

He gave judgment for the tailors. And told the man that the major defects of his suits would disappear if he slimmed.

Council ties rents to wages

RENTS of council flats and houses at Hampstead are to be based on tenants' incomes—wives and children included.

The Tory - controlled council agreed to the scheme last night, despite protests from a deputation of 150 tenants.

Rents will be fixed at one-seventh of the householder's gross earnings, plus one-seventh of his wife's earnings over 30s., plus 3s. 6d. for each child under 21 working, and 1s. 6d. for each child over 21 working.

All tenants except the old and [text cut off]

NEW TURN IN

Mystery in MacE

From THOMAS CLAYT

SOME news came Commissioner I wreck of the Kanga look which Claude throughout the film

For the Cannes poli confirmed that Fredd MacEvoy's yacht Kangaro had a passenger aboar when she sailed from th Riviera on her last trip

The passenger was American.

The three survivors at f denied there had been passenger. Confronted w police evidence today, howev survivor Willy Gehring admitt it.

A 'GRILLING'

He said the American left t yacht at Ibiza—which is the po of the Balearic island of t same name, 80 miles east Spain.

Leandri called on Praxmar the survivor who is wanted murder by the Austrian poli And

seven hours, the Palais Justice at M rakesh. Pr marer w grilled afres Back Rabat Pie Deville. Fren Morocco's N policema flicked a g through MacEv dossier. He said : the infor tion we h

That look of **CLAUDE RAINS**

harvested about MacEvo his crew has been sent dail Paris and Scotland Yard been kept right in the pictu "We have been told not release the results of inquiry here.

UNDESIRABLES

On this front page of the *Daily Express*, a British newspaper, Herbert Mills gets the attention he had wanted for so long. His father claimed that the boy was bitter due to having to undergo 13 years of painful treatment for a birth defect.

He described how he had met Mabel for the first time at the movies and then arranged to see her again the following evening. He was obsessed with the idea of committing the perfect murder, and since this seemed the perfect opportunity, he took her to the orchard and killed her.

But he became impatient when it took too long for her body to be found. He wanted to gloat over the inability of the police to bring him to justice, as had Leopold and Loeb.

The prosecution had good forensic evidence. Head hairs from Mills were found on Mabel Tattershaw's body, and a thread from his suit had lodged under one of her fingernails as she fought for her life. Herbert Mills was convicted of the murder and hanged on December 11, 1951.

TEENAGE GIRLS WHO KILLED

Thirty years after Leopold and Loeb committed their dreadful crime, another youthful pair became locked in an intense friendship that led them to murder. This time, it was two young girls who lived in New Zealand: 16-year-old Pauline Parker and 15-year-old Juliet Hulme.

Pauline Parker's mother, Mrs. Honora Mary Parker, thought the relationship had become too close and tried to break it up. Then Juliet's father decided to take his daughter to South Africa. The girls made plans for Pauline to go as well, but realized that Mrs. Parker would probably stand in their way.

On June 22, 1954, Pauline and Juliet ran into a park teashop, crying out hysterically that Mrs. Parker was dead. She had fallen and hit her head on the sidewalk, they said. (It was shown later that Pauline's mother had 45 separate wounds on her head.) The girls claimed that her head must have bumped on the ground while they were dragging her along to get help.

After long questioning, Pauline admitted that they had killed her mother with a half-brick secreted inside a stocking. Juliet claimed at first that they had only intended to frighten her into giving permission for Pauline to go to South Africa. But Pauline's diary told a different story:

"Why could not Mother die?" she had written. "Dozens of people, thousands of people, are dying every day. So why not [M]other and Father, too?" Further on, she had described how they should make it look like an accident and what weapon they should use.

Defense counsel at their trial in Christchurch pleaded that the girls were **paranoid** and insane. But the girls, who showed no remorse, were found guilty of murder and sentenced "to be detained during Her Majesty's Pleasure."

In practice, this punishment, which is used for juveniles, means that they may be given their freedom when the authorities decide it is safe to release them. Pauline Parker and Juliet Hulme were released in 1958.

Melanie Lynskey as Pauline Parker and Kate Winslet as Juliet Hulme in *Heavenly Creatures*, a 1994 movie based on the murder of Pauline's mother by the girls in 1954.

The German Carpenter

On the evening of March 1, 1932, the first indication that anything was wrong at the luxurious New Jersey estate of Colonel Charles Lindbergh came when the children's nurse, Betty Gow, asked Anne Morrow Lindbergh if she had taken the baby from his crib. Anne Morrow Lindbergh said she had not; neither had her husband. They rushed up to the nursery, where they found the empty crib and, on the windowsill, a ransom note demanding $50,000.

There was little chance of hiding the disappearance of 19-month-old Charles Lindbergh, Jr. from the media. On May 20, 1927, his father, Colonel Charles A. Lindbergh, made the first nonstop solo transatlantic flight from New York to Paris, becoming in the process not just world-famous but America's favorite son.

The news swept around the world. The Lindbergh estate was swamped with journalists, and their telephone line obstructed by well-wishers, hoax callers, and those wanting to help. This would have made it difficult for the kidnappers to get in touch.

There were few clues as to who had taken the child. There were no fingerprints in the nursery. The note contained a couple of spelling mistakes, which, an expert claimed, suggested that it had been written by a foreigner, probably a German, of low educational qualifications. It was signed with two interlocking circles: one red, one blue. Below the window were found smudged footprints and nearby, a chisel and sections of a crudely constructed ladder.

Left: Colonel Charles Lindbergh and his wife Anne, who shared an interest in aviation and conservation programs, seen here in flying clothes in the 1930s. Linburgh was one of America's most famous celebrities at the time his son was kidnapped.

Above: This photograph of the Lindbergh home at the time of the kidnapping shows an airplane flying overhead and the cars of journalists and state officials cramming the grounds. The Lindburgh kidnapping generated enormous press interest around the world.

If the kidnappers of our child are unwilling to deal direct we fully authorize "Salvy" Spitale and Irving Bitz to act as our go-between. We will also follow any other method suggested by the kidnappers that we can be sure will bring the return of our child

Charles A. Lindbergh
Anne Lindbergh

Above: This note shows the authorization, signed by Charles and Anne Lindbergh, allowing two gangsters, Irving Bitz and Salvatore Spitale, to act on their behalf in negotiations with the kidnappers. The infamous gangster Al Capone also offered his services.

KIDNAPPING

- "Kidnapper" is a slang term coined in England in the late 17th century for child stealers who sold their captives to U.S. plantation owners as slave labor.
- "Pressing," or "shanghaiing," was a form of kidnapping used to force men into becoming sailors when a ship needed a crew.
- A form of mass kidnapping was the capture of Africans to sell into slavery to work on the plantations in the New World and elsewhere.

The children's nurse, Betty Gow, and her boyfriend, Henry Johnsen, came under suspicion, and he was arrested.

A LEAD FINALLY APPEARS

It was not until a week later that the first lead came. A man named Dr. Condon had sent a letter to a newspaper appealing to the kidnappers' humanity and offering $1,000 of his own money for the return of the child. He received a reply from the kidnapper, signed with two circles (a detail not revealed to the public), asking him to act as go-between. When the time came, he was to put an advertisement in the newspaper saying, "Money is ready."

Condon agreed to act as go-between, and the kidnappers did contact him. The money was not yet ready, but he met one of them, a man named John, catching only a glimpse of his face.

John said he was a Scandinavian sailor and asked a chilling question, "Will I burn if the baby is dead?" However, he then claimed the baby was still alive. He also insisted that Henry Johnsen was innocent. As promised, John sent the baby's sleeping suit to Lindbergh and at the same time increased the ransom to $70,000.

The New Jersey State Police was headed by H. Norman Schwarzkopf, but Lindbergh kept him out of most of the planning.

Lindbergh himself drove Condon to the second meeting at a cemetery, where they both heard a foreign voice calling out, "Hey, Doctor, over here." Condon handed over the money (in gold certificates) and was given an envelope that contained a message saying the baby was on a "boad" anchored off Martha's Vineyard in Massachusetts. Lindbergh flew there immediately, but there was no trace of the child.

On May 12, 1932, the baby's body was found only a few miles away from the Lindbergh estate. It seemed that the child had been dead about two months.

A GOLD CERTIFICATE FOR GASOLINE

Nearly two and a half years later, on September 15, 1934, a man filled up his car at a gas station and paid using a gold certificate. These had been called in by the government, but were still being accepted as payment by shops and businesses.

As a precaution, the attendant wrote the registration number of the customer's dark-blue Dodge sedan on the back. At the bank the next day, the note was recognized as part of the ransom money.

The driver was a 35-year-old German, Richard Bruno Hauptmann, an illegal alien. After he was arrested, $14,600 of gold certificates was found

IS THIS YOUR HANDWRITING?

Handwriting identification has helped convict many criminals, even when they have been forging someone else's writing. Our handwriting becomes such a spontaneous act that it is difficult to keep up an imitation of another hand without reverting to crossing a "t" or looping a "y" in our own individual way.

stored in his garage. When he was finally brought to trial, it turned into a circus. Crowds thousands strong besieged the courthouse in Flemington, New Jersey. Outside, local boys sold souvenir miniatures of the ladder, while inside, counsel for both the prosecution and the defense were playing to the supposedly "hidden" cameras.

The prosecution claimed that the ladder had been made from wood bought at a lumberyard near Hauptmann's home, except for one rail, which had been cut from a floorboard missing from his attic. They produced a witness who identified the accused man as the one he had seen hanging around the Lindbergh estate. In addition, Condon and Colonel Lindbergh said his voice was that of "John" who had been at the cemetery.

Charles Lindbergh, Jr. was 19 months old when kidnapped. His parents released details of the baby's complicated diet program in the hope that the kidnapper might make use of the information.

A series of highly expensive experts insisted that Hauptmann's handwriting was the same as that on the ransom note, and it was shown that he misspelled words in the identical manner. The prosecution also showed that Condon's phone number had been penciled on the inside of one of Hauptmann's cupboard doors.

Edward J. Reilly defended Hauptmann. This man had the discouraging nickname of "Death House." Reilly was past his prime, had a drinking problem, and spent little time conferring with his client. Reilly pointed out that an amateur had constructed the ladder. His client, however, was a skilled carpenter. He suggested instead that members of the Lindbergh staff were highly suspect. One of the maids, Violet Sharpe, had committed suicide rather than face up to another grueling police interrogation. And, Reilly suggested, the nurse, Betty Gow, and the go-between, Condon, might have something to hide.

Hauptmann, who had a strong guttural German accent and a pompous and arrogant manner, did not make a good impression on the stand. It had already been discovered that he had a criminal record in Germany. Now, he protested that his friend, Isidor Fisch, had left the ransom money in a box in his care. Fisch, who had since died, returned to Germany in December 1933. Since Fisch owed him money, Hauptmann began to spend what was in the box.

There was strong pressure on the jury to find him guilty, and this they did. Hauptmann was executed on April 3, 1936, still protesting his innocence. Before the execution, New Jersey's Governor, Harold Hoffman, raised doubts about Hauptmann's guilt. These doubts were to keep re-emerging from various other sources afterward.

While writing his book on the case, *The Airman and the Carpenter* (1985), English investigative journalist Ludovic Kennedy discovered that Hauptmann's statements about Fisch were true. As for that telltale ransom money, it had been selling freely at a discount in the New York underworld, and it was quite feasible that Fisch had bought some.

Here, Bernard Richard Hauptmann is arrested and handcuffed on suspicion of the kidnapping and murder of Charles Lindbergh, Jr. Hauptmann had paid for gas with one of the gold certificates that was used to pay the ransom.

This photograph shows the younger Hauptmann. He was to enter the U.S. illegally after fleeing from Germany to avoid serving a second prison term for armed robbery and burglary.

BAD SPELLING CAN BE THE DEATH OF YOU

Richard Hauptmann is not the only man to have been convicted of murder for spelling English in a "foreign" manner. In 1917, a package containing a female torso and arms was found in Bloomsbury Square in London. Written on the brown paper wrapping were the words, "Blodie Belgin." World War I meant that there were many Belgian refugees in London at this time, and this may have been an effort to make the killing appear to be a reaction against them.

The laundry mark on the sheet around the remains led police to the home of Frenchwoman Emmeliene Gerrard, who had been missing for several days. Then the trail led to her lover, a Belgian butcher by the name of Louis Voisin.

He was asked to write down the words "Bloody Belgian" and did so in the way found on the package. This, as well as other evidence, such as the discovery of the victim's head and hands in his cellar, led to Voisin's conviction for murder and his execution. It seems likely, however, that Voisin's other woman friend, Berthe Roche, had actually committed the crime. She had grown jealous when she found out about her rival, although Voisin insisted that Berthe had not been involved. She was convicted of being "an accessory after the fact" and sentenced to eight years in prison, where, two years later, she became insane.

Kennedy sent the two handwriting samples to experts, who declared that the same person had not written them. The misspellings made by Hauptmann were ones he had been told to make by the police. A journalist had written Condon's phone number on the door as a joke, and the missing floorboard could be put down to police wanting their case to be watertight.

Clothing by which the Lindbergh baby's body was identified being displayed to members of the press at Hauptmann's trial. The child's corpse was too decayed and damaged by animals to be recognizable.

ANOTHER THEORY

Even more extraordinary were the claims made by Noel Behn in his book, *Lindbergh: The Crime* (1994). He writes that, in fact, a kidnapping may never have taken place. He suggests that Lindbergh's sister-in-law, Elisabeth Morrow, out of jealousy, could have killed the baby. Governor Hoffman, it emerged, had been informed by the family's chauffeur that the staff had been instructed never to leave the child alone with Elisabeth.

She had hoped to marry the famous man herself and had deteriorated mentally, partly out of disappointment and jealousy. When, and if, she killed the child, Behn suggests that Lindbergh felt the family would not be able to cope with the resultant scandal. So he had concocted the kidnapping story, which he was then unable to withdraw.

Here, a worried-looking Hauptmann (right) confers with his lawyer, Edward J. Reilly, toward the end of his trial at Flemington, New Jersey, on February 12, 1935.

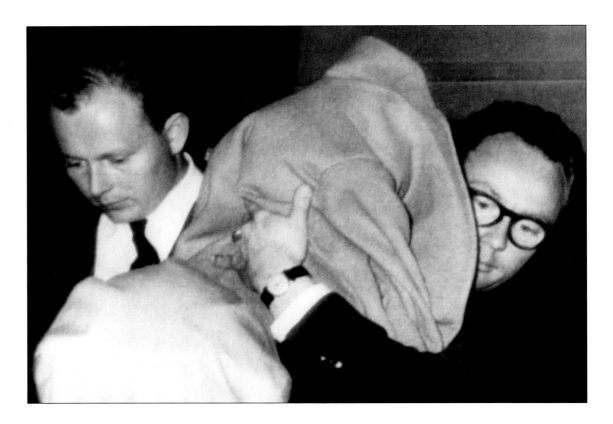

Eric Peugeot, four-year-old grandson of the French car magnate, is reunited with his father, Roland Peugeot (right), on April 15, 1960, after being found in a Paris café following his kidnapping.

MORE KIDNAPPING CASES

One of the first U.S. kidnappings took place in July 1874, when four-year-old Charlie Ross was taken from outside his home in Germantown, Philadelphia. A ransom of $20,000 was demanded from his father, a retired grocer, but it was never collected and the child was never found.

Later that same year, two burglars were shot as they left a house they had robbed. One of them confessed that they were the ones who had kidnapped Charlie Rose, but they both died before they could say what had happened to the child.

In 1899, another, somewhat bizarre, kidnapping took place, but this time with a happier ending. Twenty-month-old Marion Clarke was taken from her home in New York by trained nurse Bella Anderson, and a ransom of only $300 was demanded. This incident sparked off a frenzy in the press.

Shortly afterward, the child was recognized when Anderson took her into a grocery store. Police followed her to a farmhouse, where they arrested her, along with a couple named George and Adie Barrow.

They confessed to hatching a plot in which Anderson would take jobs caring for children, then kidnap them, but ask for only modest amounts of money. Unlike most subsequent kidnappers, instead of trying for a large sum with one snatch, they would take lots of children from less-wealthy parents and amass their fortune gradually.

The kidnappers of eight-year-old Willie Whitla, in 1909, reached for higher stakes. They asked for $10,000, but warned that the notes had better not be marked in any way. After the money had been delivered to a candy store in Cleveland, they kept their promise to let the child go.

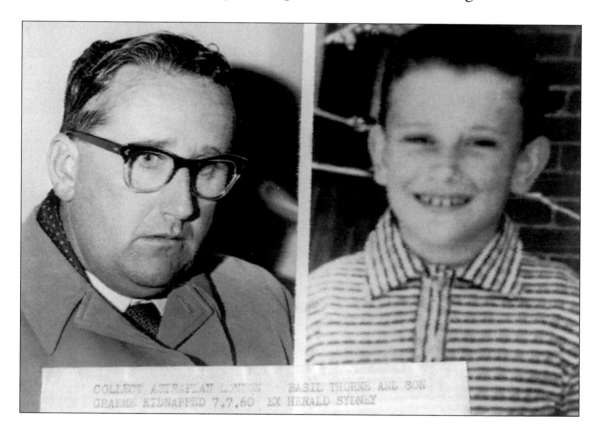

Lottery winner, Basil Thorne, and his eight-year-old son, Graeme, who was snatched from the street in Sydney, Australia, on July 7, 1960. Stephen Lesley Bradley was later convicted of Graeme's kidnapping and murder.

A few hours later, a drunken woman entered a Cleveland saloon, flashed new five-dollar bills, and ordered drinks all around. The bartender noticed that all the notes had consecutive numbers and called the police, who arrested the woman, Helen Bogle, and her husband. The rest of the ransom was found sewn inside Helen's clothes. The pair got life in prison.

During the bootleg era, when gangsters thrived, they included kidnapping in their activities, but mostly targeted wealthy businessmen rather than children. Nonetheless, the crime had reached epidemic proportions by 1932, and the Lindbergh kidnapping was the last straw. As a result, the government passed what was to become known as The Lindbergh Law. This allowed for the death penalty in certain cases and for the FBI to be called in after seven days if the victim had been taken over state lines or if the mail service had been used to make ransom demands.

THE CASE OF THE IMPOSTOR AUNT

Another crime that horrified the United States occurred in 1953. A woman claiming to be his aunt appeared at the convent school of six-year-old Bobby Greenlease in Kansas, Missouri.

She told the Mother Superior that Bobby's mother had had a heart attack and she must take the boy to her in the hospital immediately. The Mother Superior believed her. It was only a subsequent telephone call inquiring about the mother's condition that revealed she was not sick, suggesting that the boy must have been abducted.

Bobby's father was a millionaire car-dealer, and a ransom of $6,000,000 was soon demanded. The money was left in a location outside Kansas City as instructed, but the boy was not released. The kidnappers informed the parents that they were still counting the money.

A taxi driver quickly came forward to report that a drunken passenger had been talking wildly about the kidnapping. Meanwhile, police learned that an ex-convict, Carl Austin Hall, had been throwing large sums of money around.

Hall and his girlfriend were arrested and the pair quickly confessed to the kidnapping—and admitted that they had never intended to let the six-year-old boy live. Shortly after the abduction, they shot the child when he struggled as they tried to strangle him with a rope. Both were sentenced to die in the gas chamber.

Some felt the case would have been solved sooner had the FBI not been obliged to wait the **statutory** seven days before becoming involved. As a result, the Lindbergh Law was amended so that the FBI could be called in at the outset. The hope, of course, is that swifter intervention will save the lives of kidnapping victims.

Today, kidnapping has reached a new, political dimension. Terrorists and pressure groups are committing the crime to **extort** money for their causes or to gain concessions from authorities, such as the release from prison of their members.

San Diego, California: Damon Van Dam and his wife Brenda in front of journalists after the arrest of their neighbor, David Westerfield, on a charge of kidnapping and murdering their seven-year-old daughter, Danielle, on February 1, 2002.

Sacco and Vanzetti: A Case that Rocked the World

At first, this trial seemed like a run-of-the-mill payroll robbery, although a particularly cold-blooded one. However, it was to develop into what a **New York Times** *journalist termed "a case that rocked the world."*

It began on April 15, 1920, in the small town of South Braintree, Massachusetts. Paymaster Frederick Parmenter and guard Allessandro Berardelli were carrying two boxes containing $16,000 worth of wages into the Slater and Morrill shoe factory.

Two men were loitering near the entrance. Suddenly, one of them drew a gun and shot Berardelli. Parmenter dropped his box and ran, but was also shot down. Meanwhile, the second gunman stood over Berardelli and pumped more shots into him. Both men died.

The gunmen picked up the boxes and carried them to a waiting car, a stolen Buick, where several other men were waiting. It then drove off at a high rate of speed.

Police later learned that a man named Boda had been seen in that particular car, which was thought to have been used in an earlier attempted

Left: Twelve thousand workers gathered in Union Square, New York City, to protest against the execution of Sacco and Vanzetti. The controversial execution was scheduled for the following day, August 10, 1927.

Here, police officers lead away the handcuffed anarchists Bartolomeo Vanzetti (left) and Nicola Sacco (right), after their arrest for the murder of payroll guards in South Braintree, Massachusetts, on April 15, 1920.

payroll robbery. Boda escaped, but two of his associates, 29-year-old shoemaker Nicola Sacco and 32-year-old fish salesman, Bartolomeo Vanzetti, were captured.

They answered the description of the killers in that they were foreign-looking, probably Italian, and one had a walrus moustache. The men insisted they did not own guns, but both were found to be armed. In fact, Sacco's handgun was a Colt .32—the same caliber as bullets recovered from the victims.

A witness to the earlier attempted robbery picked out Vanzetti as one of the guilty men, and he was tried and sentenced to 10 to 15 years in prison. Then, both he and Sacco were also charged with the South Braintree robbery and killings. Crucial to the prosecution's case was the allegation that Sacco's gun was one of the murder weapons.

THE SIEGE OF SIDNEY STREET

In 1911, another anarchist incident took place in London, England, which terminated in the famous Siege of Sidney Street. This incident began when a group of Russian anarchists were disturbed while robbing a jeweler's in London's East End. They shot five policemen. One was killed on the spot, while two others died later as a result of their wounds.

Several of the fugitives escaped, but police learned that two of them had taken refuge in a house in Sidney Street—and a siege began. Police firepower was puny in those days—four policemen and two bystanders were wounded—so the army was brought in to resolve the situation.

Eventually, the stalemate was ended when the house went up in flames. Two bodies were found in the ashes. One had a bullet wound, which may have been the result of incoming fire.

RIFLING

Cutting a spiral groove in a gun barrel aids in the accuracy of a bullet's flight and extends the range of bullets fired. Gun manufacturers cut grooves to different specifications for each gun type.

The direction of the grooves also differs. Some are directed to the left, some to the right. In addition, each gun acquires its own "fingerprint" through variations in the grooves. Some are acquired in manufacture and others are caused by wear and tear.

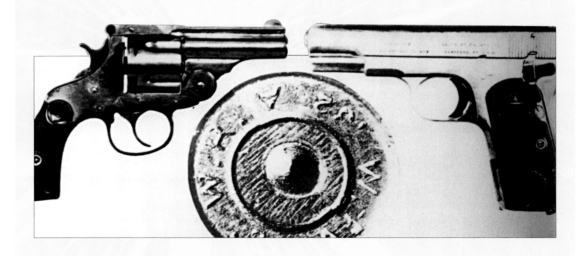

THE EARLY DAYS OF BALLISTICS

The science of ballistics was still in its infancy, and experts did not yet have the benefit of a comparison microscope. Nonetheless, a prosecution witness testified that it was Sacco's gun that fired bullets found in the victims; another said it could have been the gun; and two defense experts declared it could not be the gun.

Both sides produced a mass of identification witnesses, who naturally contradicted each other and caused great confusion. However, the two men were eventually found guilty and sentenced to death.

The case drew international attention. Appeals and protests flooded in

This painting of Vanzetti and Sacco was produced by Lithuanian social realist artist Ben Shahn (1898–1969), also an immigrant to the United States. Shahn produced several critical works on the plight of the pair.

from left-wing parties around the world, who declared that this was a typical example of capitalist injustice. Petitions for **clemency** were signed by famous figures, including Albert Einstein, George Bernard Shaw, and H.G. Wells. Sympathizers raised funds for a retrial, and years of appeals and stays of execution followed.

A new trial was never granted, but in July 1927, a three-man committee was appointed to reexamine the case. By this time, the New York Bureau of Forensic Ballistics had been established, and one of its team, Calvin Goddard, brought along a comparison microscope that they had developed.

Bartolomeo Vanzetti and Nicola Sacco pose for a photograph. This photograph became world-famous at the time, and was used by artist Ben Shahn for drawing portraits and other depictions of the pair (see page 55).

With this, two slides could be viewed alongside each other so that the **rifling** on the bullet found at the scene of the crime could be compared with one fired from the suspect gun. Goddard demonstrated to the satisfaction of the committee that Sacco's gun was the murder weapon. The verdict was considered to be safe.

APPROACHING EXECUTION

The date for their execution was set for August 10, 1927. As the time approached, there were protest marches and demonstrations around the globe, from London to Tokyo. Strikes were called in Brazil, Czechoslovakia, and Switzerland. Bombs exploded in Sofia (the capital of Bulgaria) and Paris. The U.S. flag was burned in Casablanca, and the Chicago police had to disperse a mob of 4,000 using tear gas and gunfire.

The protests were halted when, on August 10, a further 12-day respite was granted for an appeal. Meanwhile, the home of one of the jurors on the case was bombed when he declared his belief that the sentence was just and should be carried out.

The final appeal was rejected on August 19, and the two men were executed just four days later, on August 23. As a result, there was a strike in Argentina, rioting broke out in Geneva, and police in Copenhagen had to resort to using clubs to scatter marchers. Furthermore, the turmoil and street fighting on the streets of Paris, reported Louis Stark of the *New York Times*, were such as had not been witnessed since World War I. All told, hundreds of protesters were arrested around the world. There were many injuries and some deaths.

Even many Americans who believed that Sacco and Vanzetti were guilty were nonetheless uneasy about Judge Thayer, the man who presided over all these proceedings and who had made no secret of his prejudice against "these **anarchist** bastards." People felt embarrassed by his conduct at the trial and during the subsequent retrial rejections.

In 1977, Michael Dukakis, the governor of Massachusetts, issued a

The funeral procession of Sacco and Vanzetti at North End, Boston's oldest residential district, was attended by thousands even though police had attempted to limit the numbers to prevent further disturbances.

proclamation removing any stigma and disgrace from the names of Sacco and Vanzetti. He acknowledged that the two men had been denied a fair trial and declared the 50th anniversary of their death to be a day of commemoration.

Here, the anarchist Unabomber, Theodore Kaczynski, is led away by a police officer, under arrest in January 1998. Unlike Sacco and Vanzetti, who were thought to have killed to obtain funds, he sent bombs to make a political protest.

THE TOTTENHAM OUTRAGE

In some respects, this event was similar to the Sacco and Vanzetti affair. It took place in North London in January 1909. Two armed, Latvian anarchists, Paul Hefeld and Jacob Lepidus, lay in wait for Albert Keyworth, a 17-year-old clerk, who was bringing the week's wages to Schnurmann's rubber factory.

As the boy got out of the car, the anarchists went to snatch the money, but Albert put up a fight, as did the driver, who was shot several times. Another man who came to their aid was also hit. The attack was not well planned. Not only did it take place right across the street from a police station, but the victims (who miraculously suffered only minor injuries) had a vehicle with which to pursue the bandits, who fled on foot.

Two policemen, Constables Newman and Tyler, rushed out of the station and jumped on board the car. They quickly caught up with Hefeld and Lepidus, who fired at the car, putting it out of action and mortally wounding a 10-year-old boy in the process. The pursuers continued the chase on foot despite the fact that their quarry turned around every now and then to fire at them. Police Constable Tyler received a bullet in the head and died soon after reaching the hospital.

The chase carried on for another four or five miles, with the fugitives commandeering in turn a tram (a streetcar), a milk cart, and a van. Eventually, they were faced with a dead end. To continue their flight, they would have to climb a high fence. This was too much for the exhausted Hefeld, who was shorter than his comrade. As his pursuers closed in, he shot himself. The wound was not instantly fatal, however, and he died in a hospital three weeks later.

By now, the crowd of pursuers included two armed policemen and duck hunters from the nearby Tottenham Marshes. Lepidus crossed some fields, burst into a workman's cottage, and ran upstairs. As police closed in, he also shot himself.

John George Haigh: The Acid-Bath Murderer

Many murderers have been under the illusion that if a body is not found, they cannot be charged. Such a one was John George Haigh.

In February 1949, the mostly well-to-do guests in the Onslow Court Hotel in London began wondering what could have happened to their fellow resident, Mrs. Olivia Durand-Deacon. Two of them, Mrs. Constance Lane and John George Haigh, were so concerned that they decided to report her disappearance to the police.

Haigh revealed to female Sergeant Maud Lambourne that the missing woman had failed to keep an appointment with him the previous day. She had told him her ideas about producing artificial fingernails, and he was going to show her his place of business in Sussex, where he did his "experimental work." He was

Left: John George Haigh, 39, on his fifth appearance at magistrate's court to answer the charge of murdering Mrs. Durand-Deacon. His manic smile may have been a strategy to help prove his insanity.

Here, crowds gather to watch as a London detective carries a box of exhibits, taken from Haigh's workshop, out of the court where he is being tried for the murder of Mrs. Durand-Deacon.

eager to help find the missing woman. In fact, Haigh seemed almost too eager, and his glib manner aroused the policewoman's suspicions.

Subsequent inquiries revealed that Haigh had a long record of theft and fraud and had been to prison many times. Police therefore decided to inspect this "place of business," which turned out to be no more than a factory storeroom in Crawley, in Sussex. Here they discovered a pistol as well as a cleaning ticket for a Persian lamb coat, and this turned out

NO BODY, NO CRIME?

The Latin phrase *corpus delicti* means "the body" (that is, the substance or fundamental facts) of the crime, not the body of the victim. For a murder charge, the body of the victim is not essential, but it must be shown that:

• Death has occurred.

• The dead person has been identified as the alleged victim.

• The killing was the result of unlawful violence.

to belong to Mrs. Durand-Deacon. They also learned that he had sold her jewelry in a nearby town.

Haigh was arrested. When questioned, he came up with different stories, but then suddenly asked what the chances were of anyone being released from Broadmoor, which was a criminal lunatic asylum. Then he exclaimed, "Well, if I told you the truth, you wouldn't believe me....Mrs. Durand-Deacon no longer exists....I have destroyed her with acid." He smiled at the policeman. "How can you prove a murder if there is no body?"

HOW HAIGH DID IT

He told the police they would find "the sludge that remains" at Crawley and said, "I did the same with the Hendersons and the McSwanns."

He was right in saying that no body remained, but Mrs. Durand-Deacon's dentures had not dissolved in the vat of sulfuric acid and were identified by her dentist. Neither had her gallstones, from which she suffered, or a strap from her handbag. There were also sufficient bone fragments to prove the body was human. Furthermore, bloodstains were found on the Persian lamb coat, Haigh's shirt cuffs, and the wall of the storeroom. Haigh described how he had taken her down to Crawley to view his workshop, shot her, and then put her body in a vat of acid to dissolve.

PROOF OF INSANITY

At the time of Haigh's trial, defense pleas of insanity were based on the McNaughten Rules. Put simply, these rules stated that it must be proved that at the time of committing the offense, the accused did not know he or she was doing wrong. The rules were drawn up in 1843,

following the trial for murder of Daniel McNaughten. He had intended to kill the British Prime Minister, Sir Robert Peel, but instead shot Peel's private secretary, who later died. McNaughten's defense counsel showed that the accused was suffering from the delusion that Peel was persecuting him. He was found not guilty on grounds of insanity.

The McNaughten Rules were adopted in most English-speaking countries (one exception is Scotland). Some U.S. states have broadened them a little, and New Hampshire drew up its own. There have been attempts at redefining them to take into consideration, for example, the irresistible impulse to commit a crime even if you know it is wrong.

Today, there is more emphasis on the fact that the accused may have been suffering from "diminished responsibility" and also on the opinions of psychiatrists. However, the principal idea of the McNaughten Rules is still taken into consideration.

McSwann had been an arcade owner who had employed Haigh back in 1936. Haigh met their son, Donald, after he had come out of prison in 1943. Proposing a business deal, he invited him to a nearby workshop, where he bludgeoned him to death.

While in prison, Haigh had experimented with dissolving mice in sulfuric acid and he now did the same to Donald McSwann's body. After telling his parents that Donald had gone to Scotland, he lured each of them, separately, to the workshop. There he murdered them and took control of their **assets**.

In this press photograph of the investigation, Dr. S. Holden (center), Director of the Police Forensic Laboratory at Hendon, North London, examines the ground on which Haigh emptied the sludge that was left in his acid drums.

By 1947, Haigh was again in need of money. He pretended that he wanted to buy a house that Archie and Rose Henderson had for sale. The deal fell through, but he stayed friendly with the couple, and soon killed them in a similar manner to the McSwanns. When he met Mrs. Durand-Deacon in 1949, he had spent £7,700 gained from the Hendersons and was in search of another victim.

THE "VAMPIRE KILLER"

The motive for these killings was not monetary gain, Haigh claimed to the police, but his desire to drink the victim's blood. Clearly, now that he had been charged with murder (despite the lack of a whole body), he had decided that a plea of insanity was the best way to save himself from the gallows, and had thus come up with this fantastic tale.

In prison, he claimed that there had been more victims and told shocking tales to back up his claim to being what the newspapers were already calling the "Vampire Killer." Observers noticed that he was clearly enjoying his moment of fame.

Only one of the several medical experts who examined John George Haigh supported his plea of insanity, but the jury did not agree with him. The evidence had shown Haigh to be a cold and calculating killer who murdered for gain. He was found guilty and was executed at Wandsworth Prison in South London on August 6, 1949.

Haigh was not the first murderer to try to dissolve a human body. In 1897, the wife of Chicago businessman Adolph Louis Luetgart went missing. He insisted she had left him, but shortly prior to this, he had purchased 325 pounds (147 kg) of caustic potash—for the purpose, he claimed, of making soap with which to clean up his sausage factory.

EVIDENCE OF HUMAN REMAINS

However, Luetgart's behavior was so suspicious that his wife's brother went to the police. Eventually, the "soap" was drained, leaving behind two of his

Large crowds gathered outside Wandsworth Prison, South London, on the day that John George Haigh was hanged for the murder of Mrs. Durand–Deacon.

wife's rings, some fragments of bone, and a tooth. Expert witnesses declared the soapy substance to be flesh, which had been boiled in the caustic potash, that the bone fragments were human, and that the tooth came from Mrs Luetgart's false set.

The jury found it difficult to believe an entire body could be dissolved. They failed to agree and were dismissed. However, after a second trial was held, Luetgart was found guilty and given a life sentence. One of the most telling points against him was that he had spent $40 buying the caustic potash when $1 would have bought enough soap to clean his factory.

No traces at all of the body of actress Gay Gibson were found when she was reported missing from her cabin while returning home to England from South Africa on the liner *Durban Castle* in October 1947.

However, a night watchman reported that he had answered Miss Gibson's cabin bell at around three o'clock in the morning. When he arrived, he saw ship's steward, James Camb, in the doorway. Camb called to him that everything was all right.

At first, Camb denied ever being in the cabin, but when detectives came aboard at Southampton, he finally admitted that he had been there at eleven o'clock at night, but only to ask if Miss Gibson would like a glass of lemonade.

The police hinted that if Camb had a reasonable explanation for the woman's disappearance, this was the moment to divulge it. Camb seized the opportunity and finally admitted he had been there, on Miss Gibson's invitation. He claimed that while they were having sexual intercourse, she had a fit, foamed at the mouth, and stopped breathing. He had tried artificial respiration, then panicked when it failed, picked up her body, and pushed it through the porthole.

However, this did not correspond to something the police had found— or rather, not found. Camb claimed that Gibson had greeted him wearing nothing but a yellow dressing gown, so why were her black pajamas missing? Then there was the persistent ringing of her cabin bell. This was

THE CASE OF THE POLISH FARMERS

During and following World War II, many Polish refugees settled in Britain. Two of these, Stanislaw Sykut and Michial Onufrejczyc, bought a remote farmhouse in Wales. They did not prove successful farmers, however, and by 1953, were in serious financial difficulties.

Michial complained that Stanislaw was lazy, and Stanislaw told police that his partner had beaten him up. Stanislaw eventually decided to leave, telling Michial that he wanted £600 as his share of the property.

When Michial failed to collect his mail from the local post office, police went to the farm to investigate. They found no sign of Stanislaw, but noticed that the kitchen walls were covered in spattered bloodspots, which suggested that someone had been beaten to death.

Michial claimed that it was rabbit blood and that his partner had gone back to Poland. When it was proved that the blood was human, he changed his story, suddenly remembering that Stanislaw had cut his hand in a farm machine.

When a murder is committed in an isolated area, the chances of disposing of the body are increased. Despite not being able to find the body, Michial Onufrejczyc was charged with the murder of Stanislaw Sykut. At his trial, he was found guilty and given a life sentence.

rung for assistance as she was being attacked, the prosecution claimed at trial. The long scratch marks on Cambs' arms and the fact that he did not obtain medical assistance for the young woman also worked against him.

Blood, saliva, and urine stains on the sheets were claimed to be the

THE WRONG VICTIM

Another farm murder in which no body was found was that of 55-year-old Australian Mrs. Muriel McKay. In 1969, she was kidnapped from her London home by two Trinidadian brothers, the Hoseins. They had mistakenly assumed that she was the wife of the newspaper tycoon Rupert Murdoch. Someone with a West Indian accent made huge ransom demands. The case was greatly hampered, however, by the continued attentions of the press, which caused police to believe it might be a publicity stunt.

The telephone calls were traced to the Essex/Hertfordshire area, and eventually the Hosein brothers were traced to Rooks Farm on the county borders. No trace was ever found of Mrs. McKay, but there was speculation that her body may have been burned or fed to pigs. The Hosein brothers, found guilty of kidnapping and murder, were given life sentences for the murder, plus additional time for the other offenses.

evidence of strangulation, but the defense contended that they were the result of a fit.

It was suspected that Camb had gotten rid of the body because he believed that murder could not be proved without it. He was found guilty and sentenced to death, but escaped execution because the legality of capital punishment was then under discussion in Parliament.

A line of British policeman with dogs prod the frosty winter ground on a cold February day in 1970, as they advance slowly across a field during the painstaking search for evidence at Sleepy Hollow, Essex. The search was carried out in an attempt to solve the mysterious disappearance of Australian Muriel McKay, whose body was never found.

The Trials of Dr. Sheppard

The trial of Dr. Sam Sheppard for the murder of his wife Marilyn in December 1954 attracted immense media attention. This was not only because the accused was a doctor and the story he told about the night in question was a surprising one. Even more dramatic was the fact that a local newspaper in Cleveland, Ohio, had demanded his arrest.

"Dr. Sam" and his attractive wife Marilyn seemed to have everything. They were wealthy, had a respected position in society, a full social and sports life, a beloved seven-year-old son, and another child on the way. Then, in the early hours of Sunday, July 4, 1954, the bubble burst.

The previous evening, the couple had two friends over for dinner at their Colonial-style house, which perched on a hillside overlooking Lake Erie. After dinner, while the others watched a movie on television, Sam fell asleep on the couch. He was still asleep when, just after midnight, the other couple left to go home.

During the night, Sam claimed, he was woken by his wife's screams for help. He ran upstairs to their bedroom, where he found "a white form" standing over her bed. While he grappled with this intruder, a blow from behind knocked him unconscious.

When he came around, he found that Marilyn had been violently attacked. He ran to his son's bedroom, but found him unharmed and

Left: Here, Dr. Samuel Sheppard wears an orthopedic collar for an injury that he claimed to have received during a violent struggle with the mysterious intruder who was beating his wife Marilyn to death.

sleeping peacefully. Noises were coming from the floor below, so he ran downstairs just in time to spot a man with bushy hair going out of the back door and down the steps to the lakeside. Sam chased the man and tackled him, but was again knocked out. He regained consciousness just before dawn and found himself lying half in and half out of the lake.

Once back at the house, he realized that his wife was dead. Sheppard phoned a friend, the local mayor, John Spencer Houk, yelling, "For God's sake, Spen, come quick. I think they've killed Marilyn!" When Spen and his wife arrived, they found Sam naked from the waist up, his face and neck bruised, his trousers wet, and his manner dazed.

THE POLICE ARRIVE

Seven minutes later, the first police officer showed up, and seven minutes after that, one of Sam's brothers. Shortly afterward, another brother arrived. The brothers, who were also doctors (as was their father), examined Sam and only three-quarters of an hour after the phone call to Houk, they were ushering him away to the family-owned hospital for treatment. They asked no one's permission to do this, although they later claimed that the police had not objected.

The grieving husband was soon under sedation, and the family insisted that the police restrict their questioning to 10 minutes at nine o'clock that morning, 20 minutes at eleven o'clock, and no more than half an hour at three o'clock. Even then, the police claimed one of the brothers kept interrupting the interrogations.

Later, there was disagreement as to whether Sam had needed to be hospitalized at all. The doctor who examined him for the coroner claimed that his injuries were superficial, while the expert employed by the defense disagreed.

The police had immediately been suspicious of Sam's version of events, and it did not help that he refused to take a lie detector test—on the advice, it was claimed, of his lawyers.

This photograph shows Dr. Sheppard returning to his cell late on Friday, December 17, 1954, having been kept waiting for the jury to return its verdict. After further deliberations, it finally found him guilty on Christmas Eve.

Sam Sheppard marries Marilyn, his boyhood
sweetheart, and they become a golden couple.
She taught Sunday school at Bay Methodist
Church. He liked expensive cars, but was
stingy regarding household expenses.

There were many unanswered questions. Why, if the intruder was a burglar, had he turned the place over, but taken nothing except a vial of morphine? If he had struck Marilyn just to keep her quiet, why had he thought it necessary to strike 35 blows?

Sam had been wearing a corduroy jacket over a t-shirt when he fell asleep. Where was that t-shirt? Why had his bloodstained watch been found tucked in a duffel bag in the garden? Why were there so few fingerprints in the house, and none from strangers? If he had been lying on the beach, why was their no sand in Sam's hair?

Furthermore, it seemed odd that the Sheppard's son had not woken up during all this commotion and, if there was a stranger around, why did their dog not bark at him?

THE NEWSPAPERS DECIDE THE VERDICT

The press in Cleveland had been hinting that the influential Sheppard family was obstructing justice. Eventually, however, the newspapers did away with the hints, coming out with headlines such as, "Why Isn't Sam Sheppard in Jail?" and "Quit Stalling—Bring Him In." On July 30, 1954, the police did so and charged him with the murder.

At the trial, the defense produced some answers to the questions. The intruder had removed Sam's t-shirt while he was unconscious in exchange for his own, which was bloodstained, and the assailant had obviously been a crazed drug abuser, hence the missing morphine and the manic attack on Marilyn. As for the strange absence of fingerprints, the burglar had wiped these away to make sure his own were not left at the scene.

However, any advantage gained by this reasoning was soon lost when the prosecution produced a surprise witness. Twenty-four-year-old Susan Hayes was a slim, suntanned, laboratory technician who admitted that for the last 18 months, she and Dr. Sam had been having an affair. He had told her he was going to divorce his wife. At the inquest, he had claimed that such rumors about this affair were untrue.

On December 24, 1954, Dr. Sam was found guilty of second-degree murder and sentenced to life imprisonment.

Interest in this strange case was revived in June 1957 when convict Donald Wedler confessed to Marilyn's murder. His motive is not clear. High-profile cases attract false confessions from those of unsound mind or people eager for publicity at any price. Of course, if he was indeed telling the truth, he may simply have been feeling remorseful.

WEDLER'S STORY

Wedler, who was serving a 10-year sentence for a holdup in Florida, claimed that he had been in Cleveland on the night in question. While there, he had taken a shot of heroin, stolen a car, and gone to the Lakeside area, where he had broken into a large white house.

He had seen a man asleep on a downstairs couch, then went upstairs to a bedroom and began to search a dresser. The woman in the bed had woken up, so he had beaten her with a piece of pipe. As he fled downstairs again, he had met a man, whom he also struck with the pipe. Then he had flung the weapon into the lake and driven away. However, only part of Wedler's story fitted with that of Sheppard's, and that failed to help the doctor.

Ten years after Sheppard had been sentenced, the efforts of his family and supporters paid off. His conviction was quashed on the grounds that his trial had violated his constitutional rights on several counts, and a new trial was ordered. The judge also criticized the "massive, pervasive, and prejudicial publicity," which had made it difficult to hold a fair trial.

At the new trial, it was revealed that the forensic investigation of the crime scene had not been thorough, particularly with regard to bloodspots and splashes. One defense expert claimed that these proved that the murderer was left-handed, which Sheppard was not. This time, the jury found Dr. Sam Sheppard not guilty of the murder of his wife Marilyn.

When released, he married a wealthy German divorcée, who had helped fund his fight for a retrial. She later sued him for divorce, claiming that he

The Sheppards' home in idyllic Bay Village overlooking Lake Erie. After the murder, there was a strange absence of fingerprints inside and no sign of Dr. Sheppard's bloodstained clothing.

This photograph shows Sam Sheppard after his release with his second wife Ariane, a wealthy German divorcée. They are examining a skull—having proved his innocence, Sheppard was hoping to reestablish his career as a surgeon.

had threatened her with violence and that he habitually carried weapons, such as a pistol, knives, and an ax.

SHEPPARD REBUILDS HIS LIFE

Sam became a GP, took up all-in wrestling, and married the 19-year-old daughter of his trainer. Despite the verdict of the jury in the second trial, many people still distrusted him, and he began to drink heavily. In April 1970, Sam collapsed and died due to liver failure.

Various theories were put forward by those who thought Sam Sheppard innocent. Among them was the idea that Marilyn, who also had admirers, was killed by the jealous wife of one of these admirers.

The Sheppard case came into the spotlight once again in 1989, when window cleaner and part-time handyman Richard Eberling was found guilty of murdering a wealthy 90-year-old Lakeside resident.

In its issue of August 14, 1989, *The New York Times* reported that the Sheppards had employed Eberling as a window cleaner and he had admitted to being in the bedroom to clean the windows just two days before the murder. Indeed, blood of his type was discovered inside the house, which he had explained at the time as having resulted from a cut sustained while he was working.

PALMER THE POISONER

If Dr. Sheppard was guilty, he was unusual among medical murderers, in that most of them use poisons or drugs. It is easy to see why: they have easy access to them and know how they work.

One of Britain's most notorious medical poisoners was Dr. William Palmer of Rugeley, in Staffordshire. He murdered for money and is thought to have done away with no fewer than 14 people, including his wife, brother, mother-in-law, and several of his own children. His first victim was merely a test run—a man picked at random to see how the poison worked.

Even when suspicions were aroused, he was allowed to attend the autopsy of one of his victims and tried to walk off with vital evidence—the stomach—in a jar.

One of the forensic experts who gave evidence at Palmer's trial in 1856 was Dr. Alfred Warder. The experience may have given him ideas. In 1866,

A cheerful-looking Sheppard puffs on his extra-long-stemmed pipe during a recess in his second trial, 12 years after his first. Much to his relief, the jury found in his favor this time.

Harrison Ford as Dr. David Kimble in the 1993 movie *The Fugitive*, a film based on the life of Sheppard—as was a 1963 TV series of the same name.

Dr. Warder himself came under suspicion when his third wife, Isobel, died after showing symptoms similar to those suffered by his previous two wives just before they passed away. He committed suicide by taking poison just before the inquest jury returned their verdict that Isobel had died of aconite poisoning administered by her husband.

HAROLD SHIPMAN

One of the most murderous doctors ever was the small, bespectacled, much-loved Dr. Harold Shipman of Hyde, in Greater Manchester, England. He was convicted on January 21, 2000, of the murder of 15 of his patients, but the true number he killed over many years in practice is thought to be many more; a recent inquiry has concluded that there is reason to be suspicious about the deaths of at least 166 patients.

Shipman's victims were mainly middle-aged or elderly women who lived alone, but who did not appear to be suffering from any life-threatening illnesses. He would pay them an unscheduled home visit, persuade them they needed a shot of something, and give them a lethal injection of morphine. Afterward, he would add backdated symptoms to their computerized records to make their unexpected deaths appear less surprising if checked up on. In one case, he even gave a respectable old lady a drug habit. When suspicions were finally aroused, evidence of exactly when extra entries were made and dates changed were found recorded on the computer's hard drive. An arrogant man, Shipman was not quite as clever as he thought he was.

To this day, his motives remain unclear, but it has been suggested that he may have killed patients he was tired of treating and that he enjoyed the feeling of superiority and power this gave him. However, he did steal jewelry and small amounts of cash from their homes, and it was his clumsy attempts to get his hands on his final victim's financial assets that led at last to his discovery: her daughter quickly realized that a new will in Shipman's favor was a forgery, and went to the police.

The much-respected Dr. Harold Shipman (bearded), seen here with colleagues receiving a check for improvements to his surgery. He was later revealed to have a conviction for misappropriation of drugs, dating back to the 1970s.

SOME POISONOUS DOCTORS

DATE	NAME	VICTIMS	POISON
1856	Dr. W. Palmer (U.K.)	14	Various; antimony
1858	Dr. W.H. King (U.S.)	wife	Arsenic
1864	Dr. E. de la Pommerais (France)	mistress	Digitalis
1865	Dr. E. W. Pritchard (Scotland)	wife and mother-in-law	Antimony
1881	Dr. G.H. Lamson (U.K.)	brother-in-law	Aconitine
1887	Dr. P. Cross (Ireland)	wife	Arsenic
1881	Dr. T.N. Cream (U.S.)	mistress' husband	Strychnine
1892	Dr. T.N. Cream (U.K.)	four prostitutes	Strychnine
1892	Dr. R. Buchanan (U.S.)	wife	Morphine
1910	Dr. H.H. Crippen (U.K.)	wife	Hyoscine
1911	Dr. H.L. Clark (India)	lover's husband	Arsenic
1916	Dr. A.W. Waite (U.S.)	mother and father-in-law	Bacteria and arsenic
1947	Dr. R. Clements (U.K.)	fourth wife and others?	Morphine
1965	Dr. C. Coppolino (U.S.)	wife	Succinylcholine chloride
1975	Dr. C. Friedgood (U.S.)	wife	Synthetic opiates
1979	*Mr. P. Vickers (U.K.)	wife	CCNU anticancer drug
2000	Dr. H. Shipman (U.K.)	200+ patients	Morphine, etc.

*In Britain, consultant surgeons have the title Mr.

In 1865, Dr. E.W. Pritchard was convicted of poisoning his wife and mother-in-law using antimony (a metalic element). His crime shocked Victorian Britain because of the way in which he killed his wife in cold blood and then faked remorse afterward.

GLOSSARY

Acquitted: discharged completely from an accusation

Anarchist: one who rebels against any authority, established order, or ruling power

Asset: an item of value owned

Ballistics: the science of the motion of projectiles in flight; the study of the processes within a firearm as it is fired

Capital punishment: execution as a punishment for a person convicted of committing a crime

Clemency: tendency to be merciful and especially to moderate the severity of punishment due

Communist: a person who believes in a totalitarian system of government in which a single authoritarian party controls state-owned means of production

Extort: to obtain from a person by force, intimidation, or undue or illegal power

Extradition: the surrender of an alleged criminal by one authority (as a state) to another having jurisdiction to try the charge

Forensics: crime-solving relating to the application of science

Paranoid: having a tendency toward excessive or irrational suspiciousness and distrustfulness of others

Postmortem: an autopsy

Rifling: a system of spiral grooves in the surface of the bore of a gun, causing a projectile, when fired, to rotate about its longer axis

Statutory: authorized by the statute that defines the law

CHRONOLOGY

1843:	Trial of Daniel McNaughten.
1845:	Trial of John Tawell.
1849:	Trial of Maria and Frederick Manning.
1856:	Trial of Dr. Palmer.
1864:	Trial of Franz Muller.
1874:	Charlie Ross is kidnapped.
1897:	Trial of Adolph Luetgart.
1899:	Marion Clarke is kidnapped.
1901:	Scotland Yard introduces the first fingerprinting system.
1909:	Tottenham Outrage.
1910:	Trial of Dr. Crippen.
1911:	Siege of Sidney Street.
1917:	Trial of Louis Voisin.
1920:	Trial of Sacco and Vanzetti.
1924:	Trial of Leopold and Loeb.
1927:	Sacco and Vanzetti are executed.
1932:	Charles Lindbergh, Jr. is kidnapped.
1934:	Trial of Bruno Hauptmann.
1948:	Trial of James Camb.
1949:	Trial of John George Haigh.
1951:	Trial of Herbert Mills.
1953:	Kidnapping of Bobby Greenlease.
1954:	Trial of Dr. Sheppard; trial of Michial Onufrejczyc; trial of Pauline Parker and Juliet Hulme.
1960:	Peugeot kidnapping; kidnapping and murder of Graeme Thorne.

1964:	Second trial and release of Dr. Sheppard.
1969:	Muriel McKay is kidnapped.
1970:	Trial of the Hosein brothers.
1977:	Commemoration Day for Sacco and Vanzetti.
1996:	Trial of O.J. Simpson.
1997:	Trial of Louise Woodward.
1998:	Conviction of the Unabomber.
2000:	Trial of Dr. Harold Shipmann.
2002:	Kidnapping and murder of Danielle Van Damm.

FURTHER INFORMATION

Useful Web Sites

www.crimenews2000.com/

www.karisable.com/crime.htm

www.dmoz.org/Society/Crime/Trials

www.courttv.com/trials/famous/

www.lindberghtrial.com/

Further Reading

Avrich, Paul. *Sacco and Vanzetti: The Anarchist Background.* New Jersey: Princeton University Press, 1996.

Bak, Richard. *Lindbergh: Triumph and Tragedy.* Dallas: Taylor Publishing, 2000.

Dunne, Dominick. *Justice: Crimes, Trials and Punishments.* New York: Crown Publishing, 2001.

Geis, Gilbert, and Leigh B. Bienen. *Crimes of the Century from Leopold and Loeb to O.J. Simpson.* Boston: Northeastern University Press, 2000.

Kirwin, Barbara R. *The Mad, the Bad and the Innocent. The Criminal Mind on Trial—Tales of a Forensic Psychologist.* New York: Harper Collins, 1998.

Wilson, Colin. *The Mammoth Book of the History of Murder.* London: Robinson, 2000.

About the Author

A former officer with the Metropolitan Police in London, England, Joan Lock is an experienced writer specializing in police and criminal matters. Her nonfiction crime titles include *Lady Policeman*, *The British Policewoman*, *Marlborough Street: The Story of a London Court*, *Dreadful Deeds and Awful Murders*, *Scotland Yard Casebook*, and *Tales from Bow Street*.

Joan is also the author of four crime novels and was a regular contributor to *Police Review* magazine. She has also written dramatic plays and feature programs for BBC radio in England.

INDEX

Page numbers in *italics* refer to illustrations and captions

acid 65–70
Anderson, Bella 46–7

ballistics 9, 54–7
Barrow, Adie 47
Barrow, George 47
Behn, Noel 45
Berardelli, Allessandro 51
Bitz, Irving *36*
Bogle, Helen 48
Bradley, Stephen Lesley *47*
Briggs, Thomas 19

Camb, James 70–3
caustic potash 68–70
Clarke, Marion 46–7
Clifford, Max *8*
Condon, Dr. John F. 37–8, *39*, 40
confessions 28
corpus delicti 65
Crippen, Cora 9–12, 14–16, 18–19
Crippen, Dr. Hawley Harvey 9–19, *10*, *11*

Darrow, Clarence 28
Dew, Walter *11*, 12, 14
doctors 83, 88
drugs 16, 83, 86, *87*
Dukakis, Michael 57–8
Durand-Deacon, Olivia 63–5, *64*, *69*

Eberling, Richard 83
Einstein, Albert 55
Englund, Sven 28
extradition 21

Federal Bureau of Investigation (FBI) 48, 49
Fisch, Isidor 40
Ford, Harrison *85*
forensic evidence 9, 16, 27, 29, 30, 32
Franks, Bobby 23, *23*, 24–9, *25*, *26*

Gerrard, Emmeliene 41
Gibson, Gay 70–3
Goddard, Calvin 55–7
Gow, Betty 35, 37, 40
Greenlease, Bobby 48–9
guns, rifling 54, 57

Haigh, John George 9, *62*, 63–8, *64*, *67*, *69*
Hall, Carl Austin 48–9

handwriting 38, 40, 43
Hart, Sarah 17
Hauptmann, Richard Bruno 9, 38–43, *41*, *42*, *45*
Hayes, Susan 79
Hefeld, Paul 60
Henderson, Archie 65, 68
Henderson, Rose 65, 68
Hoffman, Harold 40, 45
Holden, Dr. S. *67*
Hosein brothers 72
Houk, John Spencer 76
Hulme, Juliet 32–3, *33*
hyoscine 16

insanity 66

Johnsen, Henry 37

Kaczynski, Theodore *59*
Kendall, Captain Henry 12–14, *14*
Kennedy, Ludovic 40–3
Keyworth, Albert 60
kidnappings 35–49

Lambourne, Sergeant Maud 63
Lane, Constance 63
le Neve, Ethel *10*, 11, 12–14, *13*, 18
Leopold, Nathan 9, *22*, 23–9, *26*, 30, 32
Lepidus, Jacob 60, *61*
Lindbergh, Anne Morrow *34*, 35, *36*
Lindbergh, Colonel Charles *34*, 35, *36*, 37–8, *39*, 45
Lindbergh, Charles, Jr. 9, 35–45, *39*, *44*, 48
Lindbergh Law 48, 49
Loeb, Richard 9, 23–9, *26*, 30, 32
London, Sidney Street Siege 53
Luetgart, Adolph Louis 68–70

McKay, Muriel 72, *73*
McNaughten, Daniel 66
McNaughten rules 66
McSwann family 65, 67
Manning, Frederick 20–1
Manning, Maria 20–1
Mills, Herbert *28*, 29–32, *31*
morphine 86
Morrow, Elisabeth 45
Muller, Franz 19–21
Murdoch, Rupert 72

Newman, Police Constable 60
Newton, Arthur 16–18

O'Connor, Patrick 20

Onufrejczyc, Michial 71

Palmer, Dr. William 83–4
Parker, Honora Mary 32–3
Parker, Pauline 32–3, *33*
Parmenter, Frederick 51
Peugeot, Eric *46*
Peugeot, Roland *46*
poisoners 16, 17, 83, 85, 88, *89*
Pritchard, Dr. E.W. *89*
prussic acid 17

Reilly, Edward J. 40, *45*
rifling 54, 57
Roche, Berthe 43
Ross, Charlie 46

Sacco, Nicola 9, *51*, *52*, 53–9, *55*, *56*, *58*
Schwarzkopf, H. Norman 38
Shahn, Ben *55*, *56*
Sharpe, Violet 40
Shaw, George Bernard 55
Sheppard, Ariane *82*
Sheppard, Marilyn *74*, 75–80, *78*, 83
Sheppard, Dr. Samuel 9, *74*, 75–83, *77*, *78*, *82*, *84*, *85*
Shipman, Dr Harold 86, *87*
Simpson, O.J. *8*
spelling 43
Spilsbury, Dr. Bernard 16
Spitale, Salvatore *36*
SS *Montrose* *10*, 12–14, *14*
Stark, Louis 57
Sykut, Stanislaw 71

Tanner, Richard 19
Tattershaw, Mabel *28*, 30–2
Tawell, John 17, *18*
telegraphy 14, *15*, *18*
Thayer, Judge 57
Thorne, Basil 47
Thorne, Graeme *47*
typewriters 9, 23, 24, 26–8

Van Dam, Brenda *49*
Van Dam, Damon *49*
Van Dam, Daneille *49*
Vanzetti, Bartolomeo 9, *51*, *52*, 53–9, *55*, *56*, *58*
Voisin, Louis 43

Warder, Dr Alfred 84–6
Warder, Isobel 86
Wedler, Donald 80
Wells, H.G. 55
Westerfield, David *49*
Whitla, Willie 47–8
wireless telegraphy 14, *15*